Old Palm City

Mapp Road Improvements

Project Vision and History

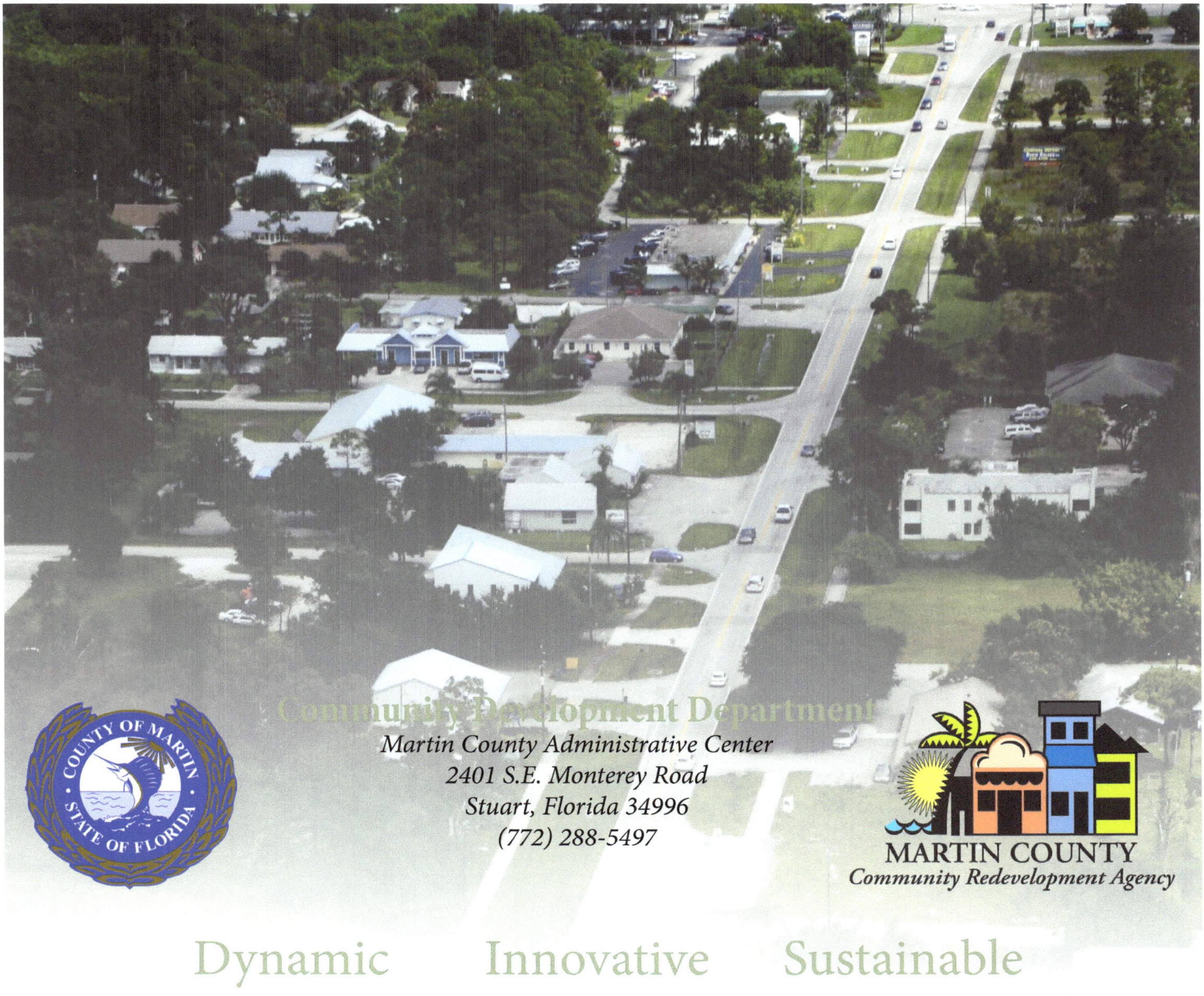

Community Development Department

Martin County Administrative Center
2401 S.E. Monterey Road
Stuart, Florida 34996
(772) 288-5497

COUNTY OF MARTIN · STATE OF FLORIDA

MARTIN COUNTY
Community Redevelopment Agency

Dynamic Innovative Sustainable

GOLDEN GATE • HOBE SOUND • INDIANTOWN • JENSEN BEACH • PALM CITY • PORT SALERNO • RIO

MARTIN COUNTY
Community Redevelopment Agency

MARTIN COUNTY BOARD OF COUNTY COMMISSIONERS

District 1	Doug Smith
District 2	Ed Fielding, Chair
District 3	Ann Scott, Vice Chair
District 4	Sarah Heard
District 5	John Haddox

MARTIN COUNTY COMMUNITY REDEVELOPMENT AGENCY

District 1	Doug Smith
District 2	Ed Fielding, Chair
District 3	Ann Scott, Vice Chair
District 4	Sarah Heard
District 5	John Haddox

COMMUNITY DEVELOPMENT STAFF

Kev Freeman, Director
Edward Erfurt, Urban Designer
Nancy Johnson, Community Development Specialist
Pinal Gandhi-Savdas, Community Development Specialist

Dynamic   Innovative   Sustainable

Reconstruction of Mapp Road
Tuesday, September 25th
Time: 6:00pm
Palm City Community Center
2701 Cornell Street, Palm City, FL

MARTIN COUNTY
Community Redevelopment Agency

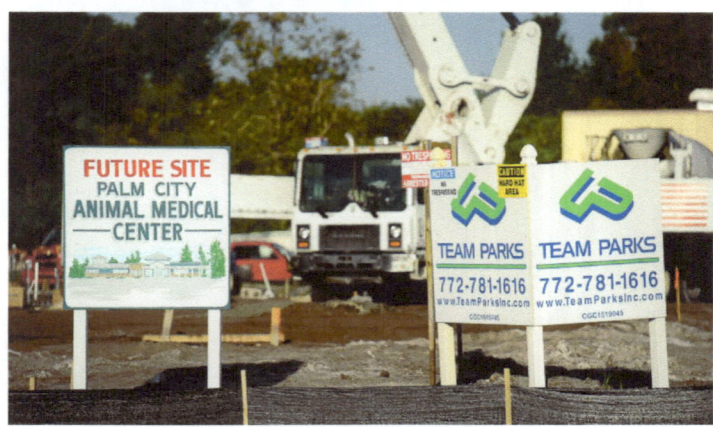

Table of Contents

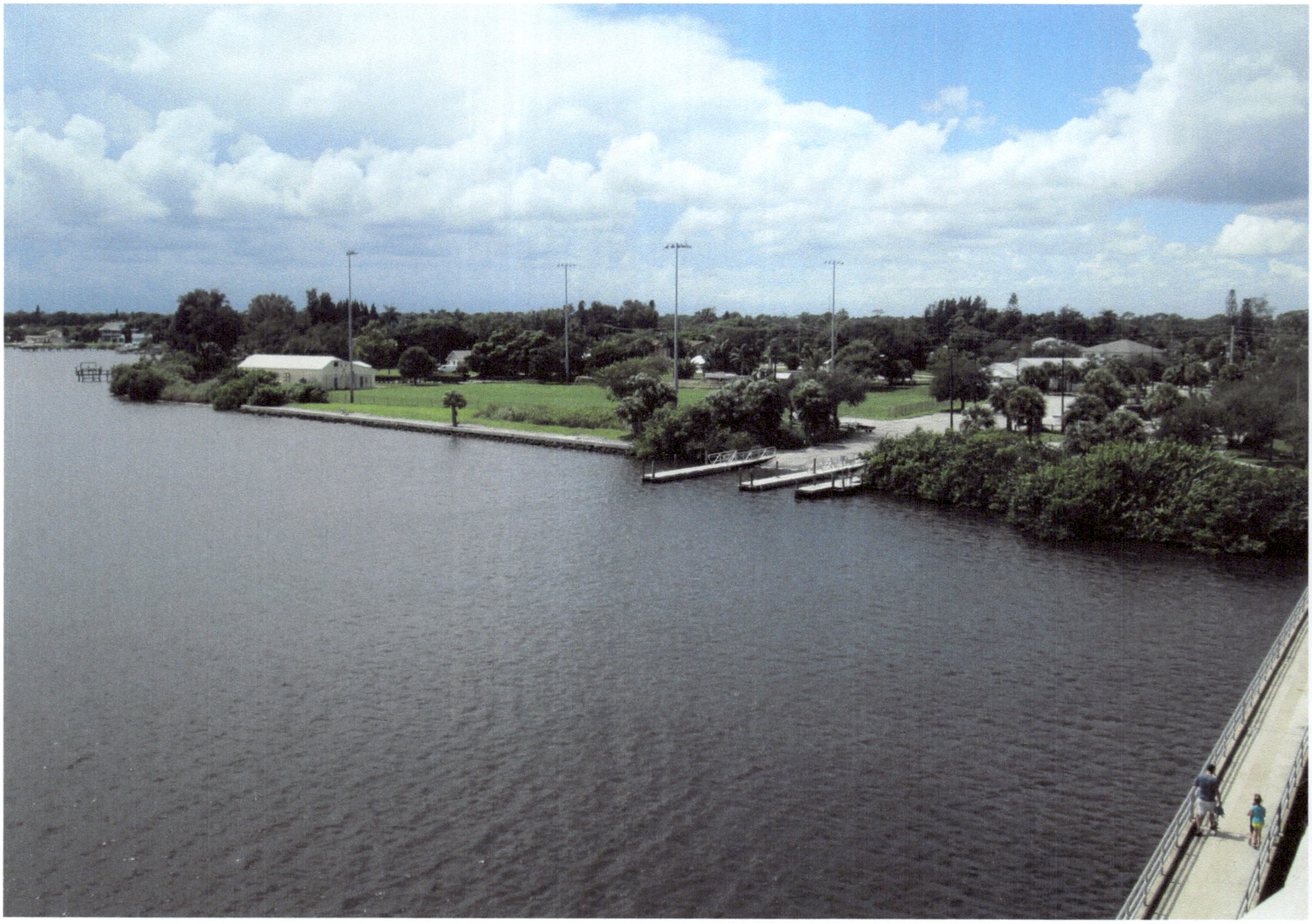

Area Summary

CRA Area: Old Palm City
Plan Adoption: April 2002
Total Area: 610 Acres
Area Highlights:
- Waterfront Community
- Home to Several Targeted Businesses

Special Designations:
- Old Palm City Community Redevelopment Area

Old Palm City

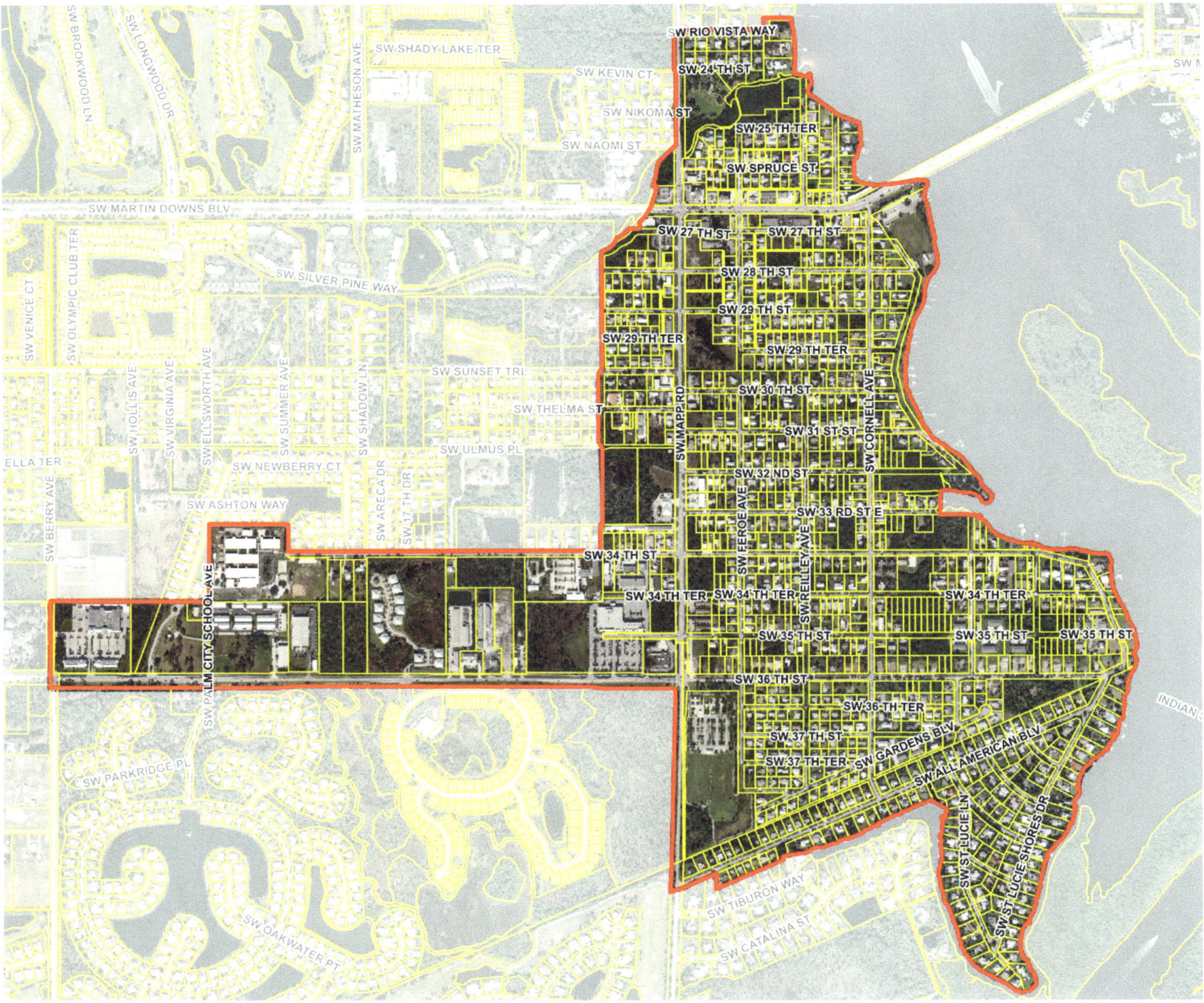

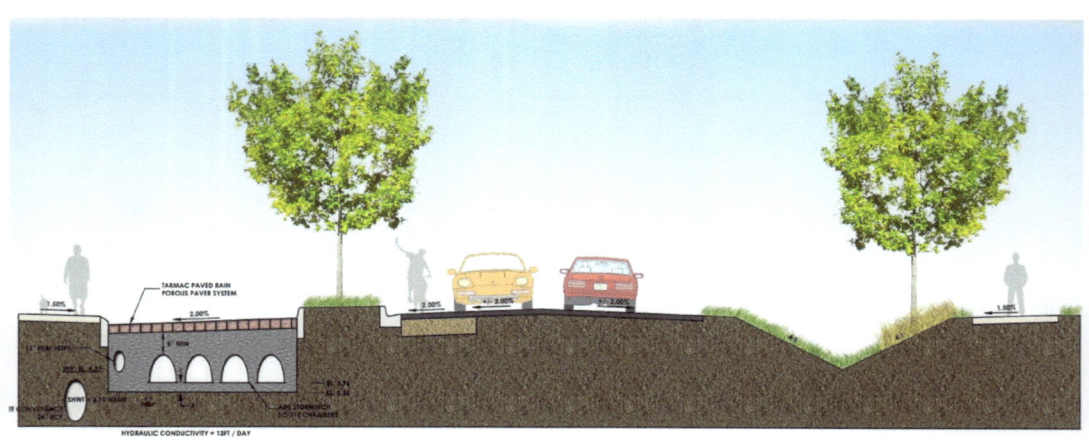

8'	17'	7'-10"			MAPP ROAD								
			4'	10'	10'	5'	3'	20'		2'	8'	2'
SIDEWALK	ACCESS LANE AND PARKING	LANDSCAPED MEDIAN									SIDEWALK	

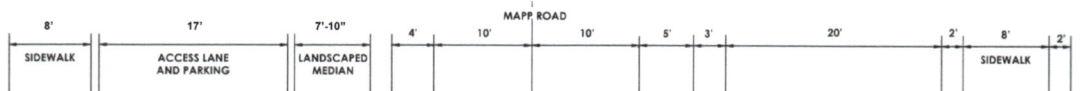

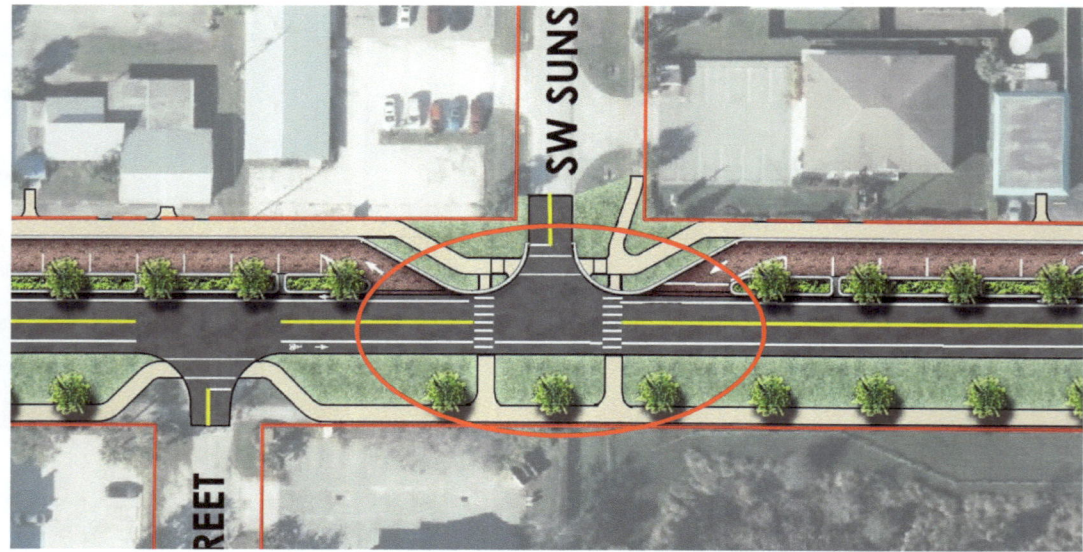

Executive Summary

Mapp Road Town Center Design

Improvements for Mapp Road as outlined in the 2003 Old Palm City Redevelopment Plan included a desire for an old-fashioned Main Street, on-street parking, and a safe, well-connected corridor that allowed for various modes of transportation including walking and biking.

The CRA began in earnest in 2008 to make this project a reality. Engineering design drawings were prepared that included parallel parking, landscaped medians, and construction of a stormwater management system capable of handling future improvements.

In 2010, the design was updated utilizing more innovative strategies such as head out angled parking to replace parallel parking stalls, and rain gardens to better incorporate best stormwater management practices and improve environmental health. Center medians were removed as a cost saving measure and a modular design approach was introduced that did not require the entire roadway to be constructed all at once.

Through a series of public workshops led by staff in 2012, the community voiced their preference for a simpler design that would allow for construction of the entire corridor, rather than a modular approach.

Staff scheduled one-on-one meetings with business owners along the corridor. The CRA received 50% design plans in August 2014. The components of the design will be prioritized in keeping with the Community's desire. With $1.3 million available in TIF for construction, the CRA will phase the project that aligns with the available TIF dollars.

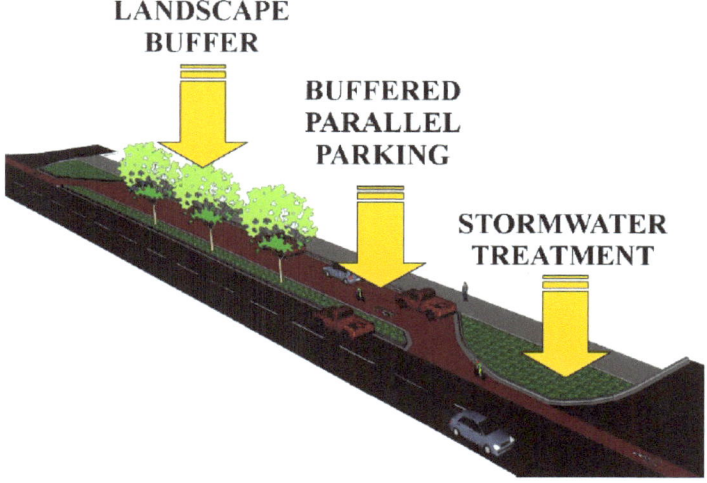

LANDSCAPE BUFFER

BUFFERED PARALLEL PARKING

STORMWATER TREATMENT

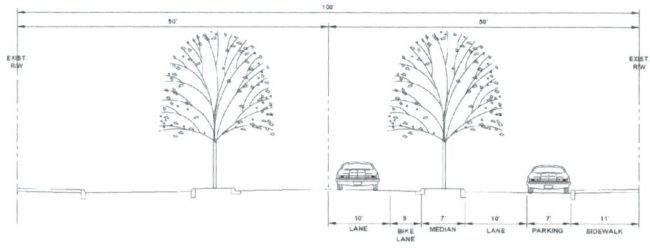

MAPP ROAD Blvd. Traditional Bike Lane Concept

Project Type:
- Complete Streets
- Innovative Stormwater Management

Funding Source:
- Tax Increment Financing (TIF)

Status:
- In Design

Project Manager: Pinal Gandhi-Savdas

6

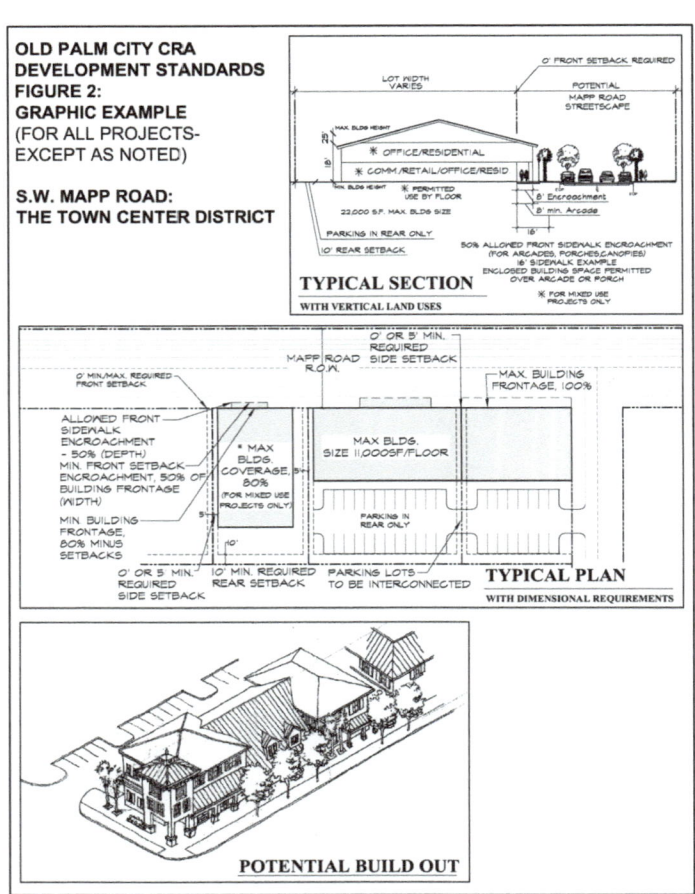

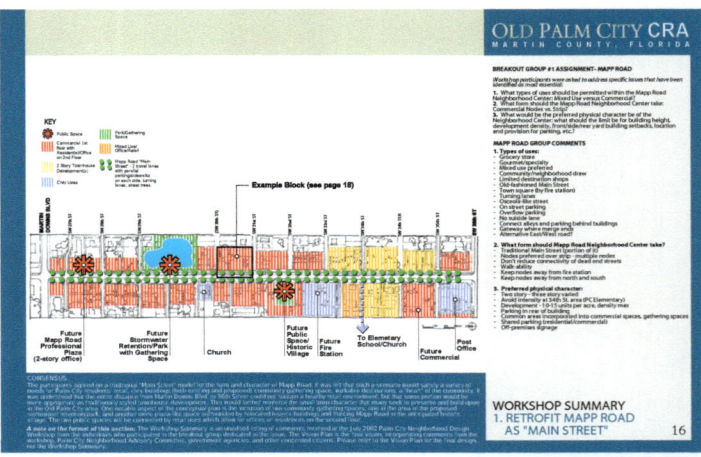

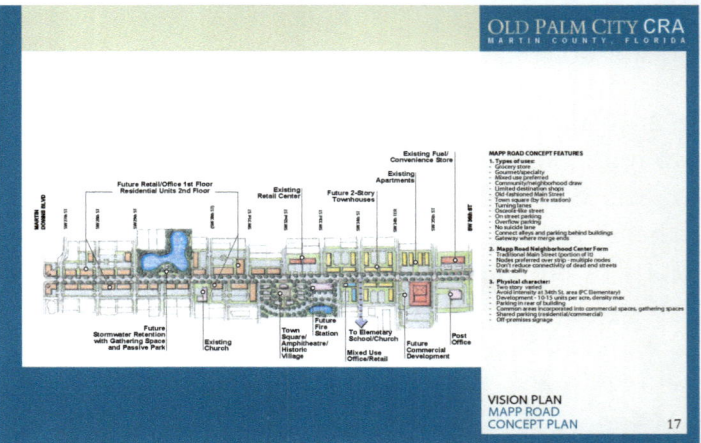

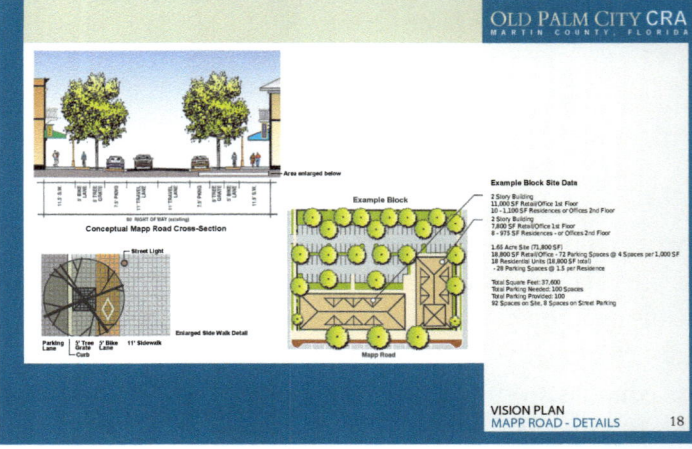

Above: Design regulations and overlay zoning requirements for Mapp Road have been adopted to implement the community vision for Mapp Road.

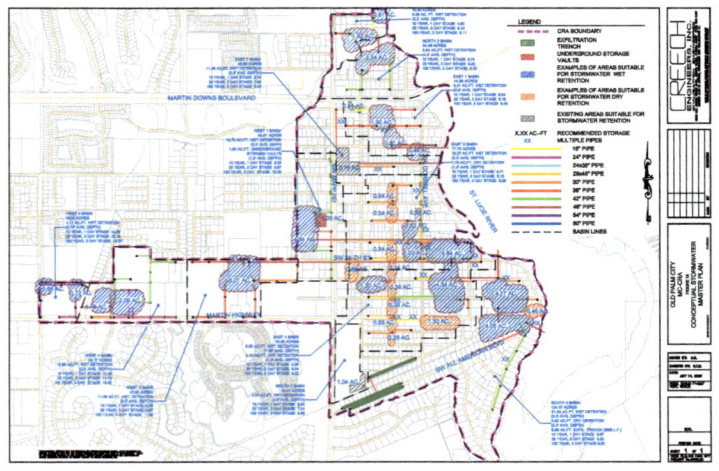

Above: Extensive planning occurred for Mapp Road with the public and the NAC in preparation of the adoption of the Redevelopment Plan.

Left: Utility and Stormwater Planning was completed for all of Old Palm City to guide priorities of projects.

Project History

Community Redevelopment Plan

The Old Palm City Community Redevelopment Area was established in 2001 by the Board of County Commissioners. The boundaries of the redevelopment area highlighted the infrastructure constraints in the older neighborhoods, the Old and New Palm City competing for commercial activity/redevelopment, the number of vacant commercial lots, and the high code enforcement activity within the Old Palm City Area.

Throughout 2002, numerous public workshops where held to seek input from the community. This information was documented and included in the Old Palm City Community Redevelopment Plan. The key issue included in the report was the proposed character and vision for the future of the Mapp Road Corridor.

The Board of County Commissioners adopted the Old Palm City Community Redevelopment Plan in April 2003. Input from workshop provided basis of components of the Redevelopment Plan. Mapp Road was proposed to be retrofitted as Old Palm City's "Mainstreet," and is detailed as a two-lane, pedestrian-friendly, mixed use corridor with on-street and shared parking; median nodes of two-story commercial and residential uses; a town square/amiphitheater/historic village, and storm water retention with gathering space and a public park.

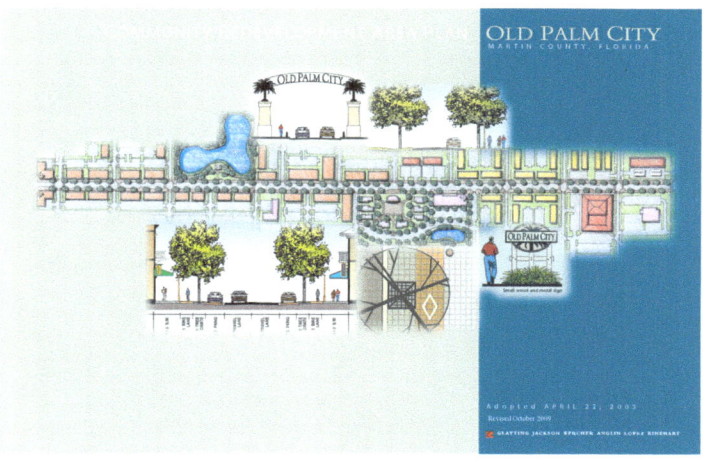

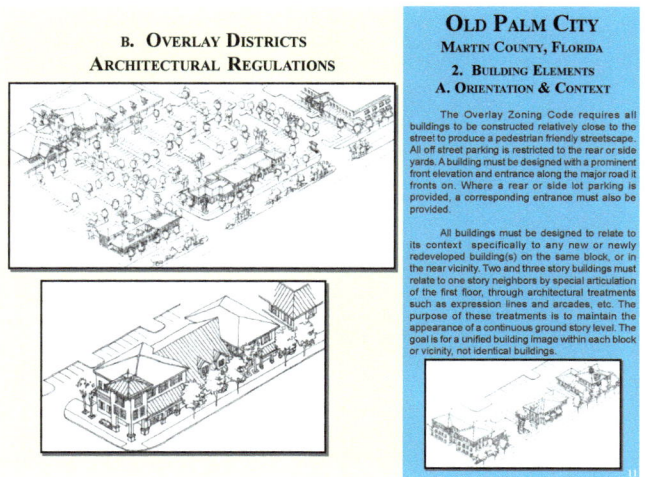

Zoning Overlays

The Board of County Commissioners adopted the Old Palm City Zoning Overlays in November 2004 which supported the community vision through the Martin County Land Development Regulations. These regulations provided the opportunity for small scale infill and mixed-use development along Mapp Road. However, the lack of infrastructure and flooding made it difficult for the redevelopment. There was also no clear idea how the county was going to manage stormwater issues in the area which led to uncertainty in future finished floor elevation requirements and road elevations, which resulted in disinterest in private investment

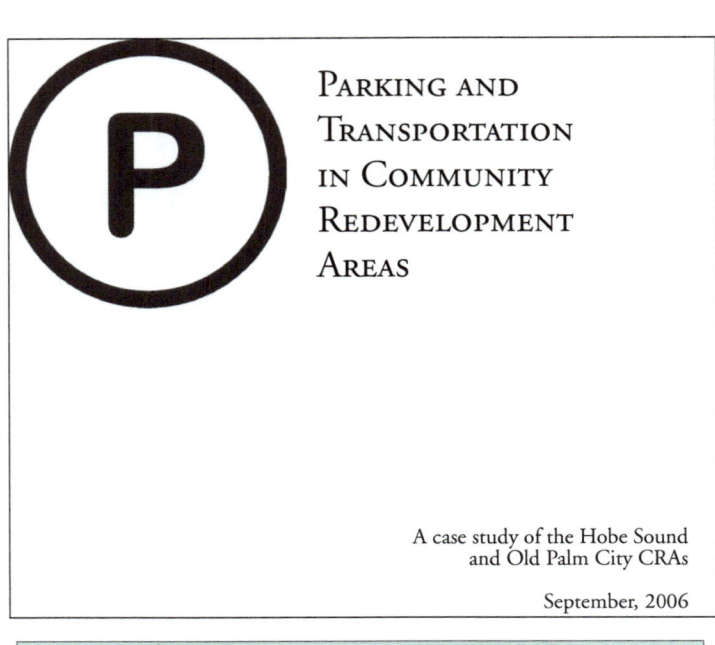

PARKING AND
TRANSPORTATION
IN COMMUNITY
REDEVELOPMENT
AREAS

A case study of the Hobe Sound
and Old Palm City CRAs

September, 2006

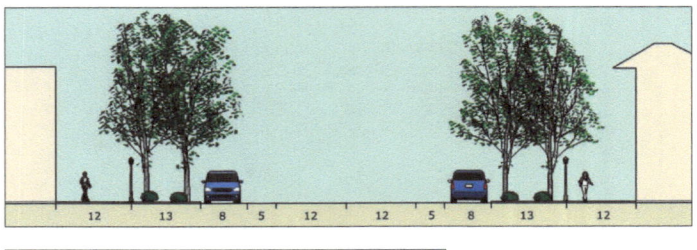

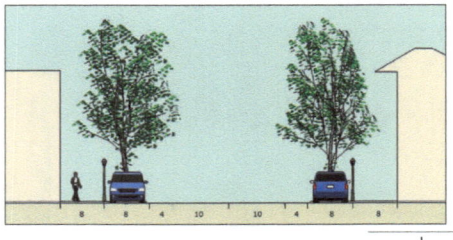

Above *Exerts from the parking study specific to the Community Redevelopment Overlays for Old Palm City, including the inventory of existing parking and possible parking configurations.*

Parking Study

In 2006, Community Development Department Staff evaluated the parking needs for the redevelopment areas following the principles promoted by famed University of California Professor, Donald Shoup. Shoup's work book "The High Cost of Free Parking," had recently been published which explains how better parking policies can improve cities, the economy, and the environment.

This report outlined a series of key elements needed to implement transportation improvements that are part of the Palm City and Hobe Sound Redevelopment Plans. Such improvements include:

- Generous sidewalks
- Shade trees, benches, and awnings to make the sidewalk more inviting
- Less on-site parking and less of it visible from the main street
- More on-street parking, shared parking among several businesses, parking lots and parking garages
- Encourage more people to walk or bicycle to the downtown area
- Encourage people to park once and walk to multiple stores or offices
- Encourage more compact development and discourage the unnecessary use of increasingly valuable land for surface parking.

The parking study also highlighted the need to create a unified parking code with shared and reduced parking rates for redevelopment, the establishment of a parking trust fund, and utilizing public rights of way for on-street parking to meet redevelopment parking requirements.

This report was shared with the Neighborhood Advisory Committees, local businesses, and local chamber of commerce. These ideas were also implemented into the Martin County Land Code, and utilized in the redevelopment of parcels in the Community Redevelopment Areas.

Utilities and Stormwater Master Plan

The Community Redevelopment Agency recognized that the lack of public utilities continued to be the biggest deterrent for redevelopment in the redevelopment areas.

In 2006, the Community Redevelopment Agency completed the Utilities and Stormwater Master Plan for Old Palm City which included a conceptual design and cost to complete all the necessary utilities and stormwater improvements for Old Palm City.

This Master Stormwater/Utility Plan provides guideline for construction and funding of infrastructure improvements necessary to meet the needs of Old Palm City in accordance with the Community Redevelopment Plan and the Neighborhood Advisory Committee's vision for the future for Mapp Road.

In 2007 the Mapp Road improvements of the stormwater and utilities master plan was identified as the top priority for Old Palm City.

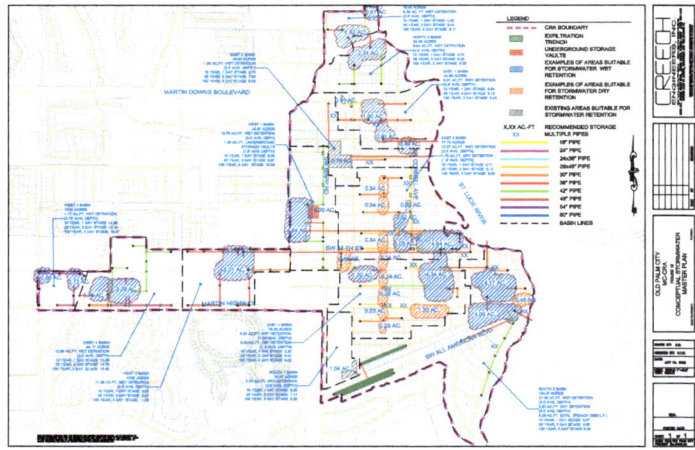

NOW Visioning

In 2009, the Community Development Department hired a new Director, Kev Freeman. He began a series called the Neighborhood Opportunities Workshop (NOW) Visioning. These two day public workshops provided the residents, property owners, and business owners of the community redevelopment area a venue to share the strengths, weaknesses and opportunities of their community. This public input built consensus on the Recommended Activity Focus areas.

The residents of Old Palm City focused on two activity focus areas; Mapp Road and the Waterfront. Residents overwhelming wanted to see Mapp Road transformed in a context sensitive street.
The Community confirmed that CRA Activity Focus should be maintained towards the implementation of the Mapp Road Retrofit. Grant opportunities have been identified that would facilitate a context sensitive street design together with a sewer system expansion. Activity Focus should also be placed on the desire to better utilize the waterfront and the Jock Leighton Park area. Partnerships between the public and private sectors should be sought, together with grant opportunities that would provide opportunities to revitalize the park area.

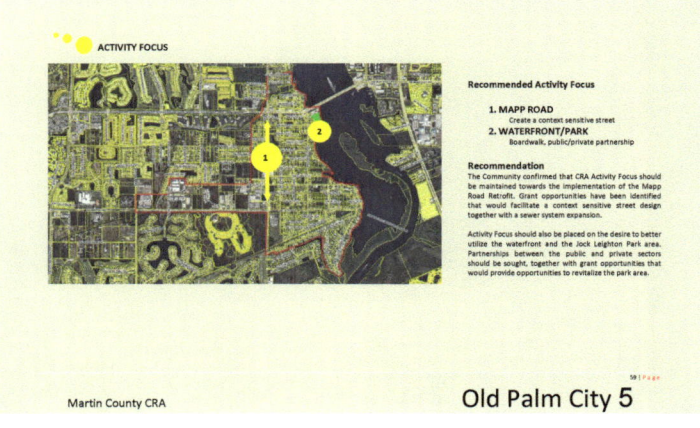

CAFE
SALON

OLD PALM CITY CRA
MARTIN COUNTY, FLORIDA

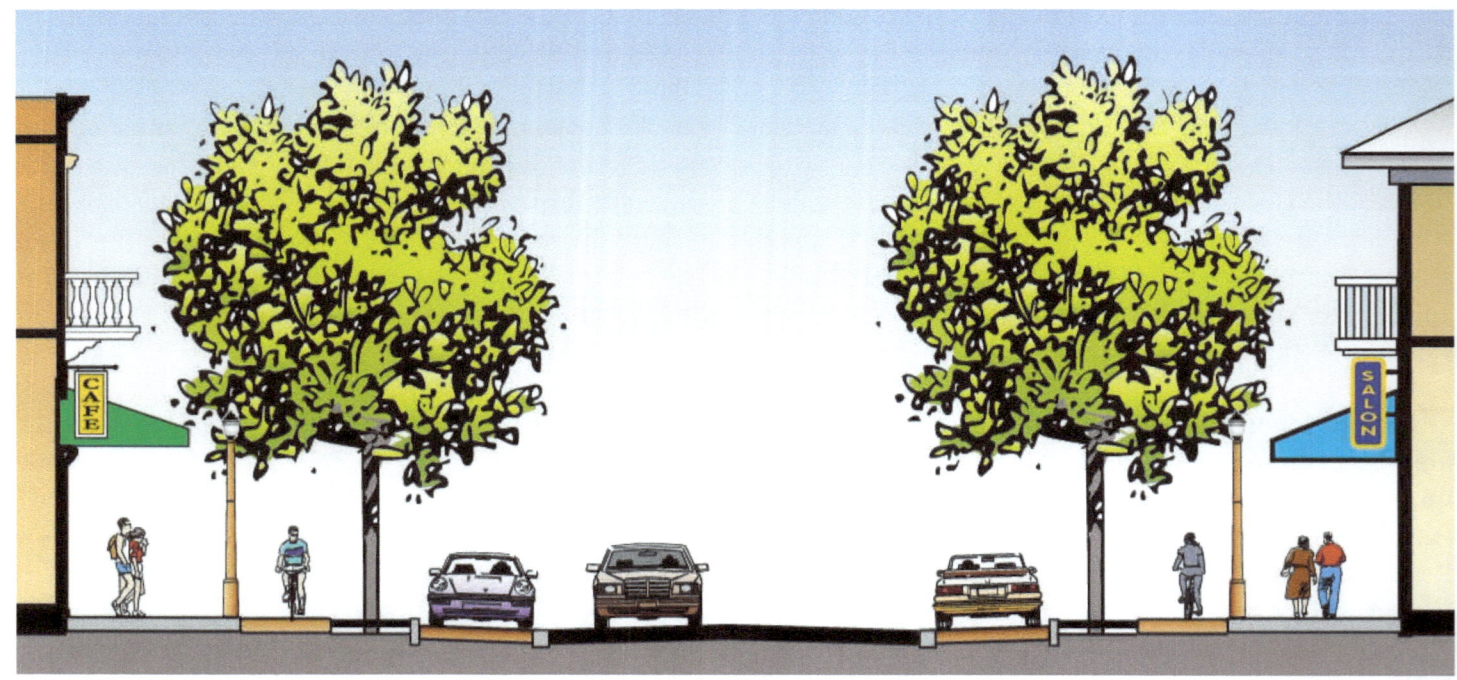

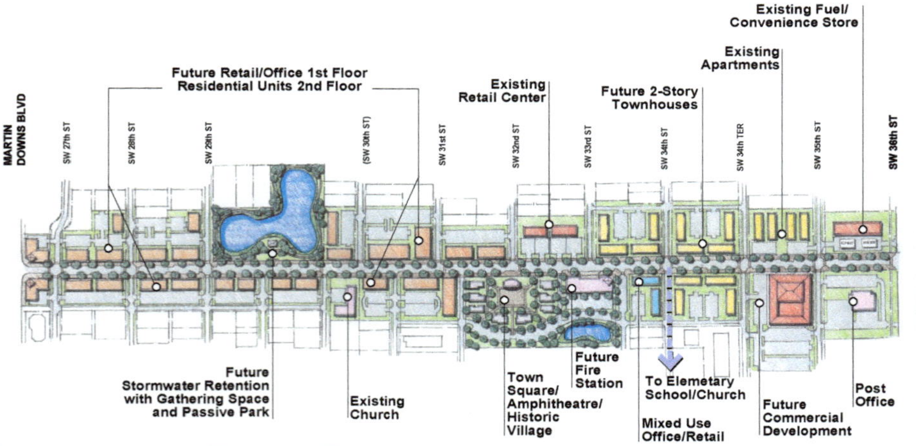
Existing Fuel/
Convenience Store
Existing
Apartments
Future Retail/Office 1st Floor
Residential Units 2nd Floor
Existing
Retail Center
Future 2-Story
Townhouses
MARTIN
DOWNS BLVD
SW 27th ST
SW 28th ST
SW 29th ST
(SW 30th ST)
SW 31st ST
SW 32nd ST
SW 33rd ST
SW 34th ST
SW 34th TER
SW 35th ST
SW 36th ST
Future
Stormwater Retention
with Gathering Space
and Passive Park
Existing
Church
Town
Square/
Amphitheatre/
Historic
Village
Future
Fire
Station
To Elemetary
School/Church
Mixed Use
Office/Retail
Future
Commercial
Development
Post
Office

MAPP ROAD CONCEPT FEATURES

1. Types of uses:
- Grocery store
- Gourmet/specialty
- Mixed use preferred
- Community/neighborhood draw
- Limited destination shops
- Old-fashioned Main Street
- Town square (by fire station)
- Turning lanes
- Osceola-like street
- On street parking
- Overflow parking
- No suicide lane
- Connect alleys and parking behind buildings
- Gateway where merge ends

2. Mapp Road Neighborhood Center Form
- Traditional Main Street (portion of it)
- Nodes preferred over strip - multiple nodes
- Don't reduce connectivity of dead end streets
- Walk-ability

3. Physical character:
- Two story varied
- Avoid intensity at 34th St. area (PC Elementary)
- Development - 10-15 units per acre, density max
- Parking in rear of building
- Common areas incorporated into commercial spaces, gathering spaces
- Shared parking (residential/commercial)
- Off-premises signage

VISION PLAN
MAPP ROAD
CONCEPT PLAN

17

Mapp Road

Following the Plan

In accordance with the vision in the adopted Old Palm City Community Redevelopment Plan, and the recommendations of the Master Utilities and Stormwater Master Plan, the Community Redevelopment Agency began the planning and design work for the implementation of Mapp Road.

The magnitude of this project required a phased approach. The most critical issue for the project was the design of the stormwater management system. In July 2008 the Community Redevelopment Agency contracted with Boyle Engineering Corporation (Acquired by AECOM) to prepare roadway design for Mapp Road which included, design, construction documents for water quality/water retention facilities, and anticipated roadway elevations. (Contract for $400,000)

In May 2009 a master permit application was submitted to South Florida Water Management District (SFWMD) This master stormwater permit included a conceptual design for the roadway, and assumed the stormwater treatment need based on impervious ROW for the entire length of Mapp Road. This permit and design could be modified as portions of Mapp Road were designed and constructed.

TIGER II Grant Application

In July 2010, the Community Redevelopment Agency applied for Tiger II Grant from the Federal Department of Transportation for $11.5 million. This grant would have provided funding for all of the improvements on Mapp Road corridor and fund the expansion of utilities to the residential neighborhood. This grant illustrated the complexity and cost when retrofitting existing neighborhoods, and the need for completed engineering drawings for these applications. The CRA was not awarded this grant.

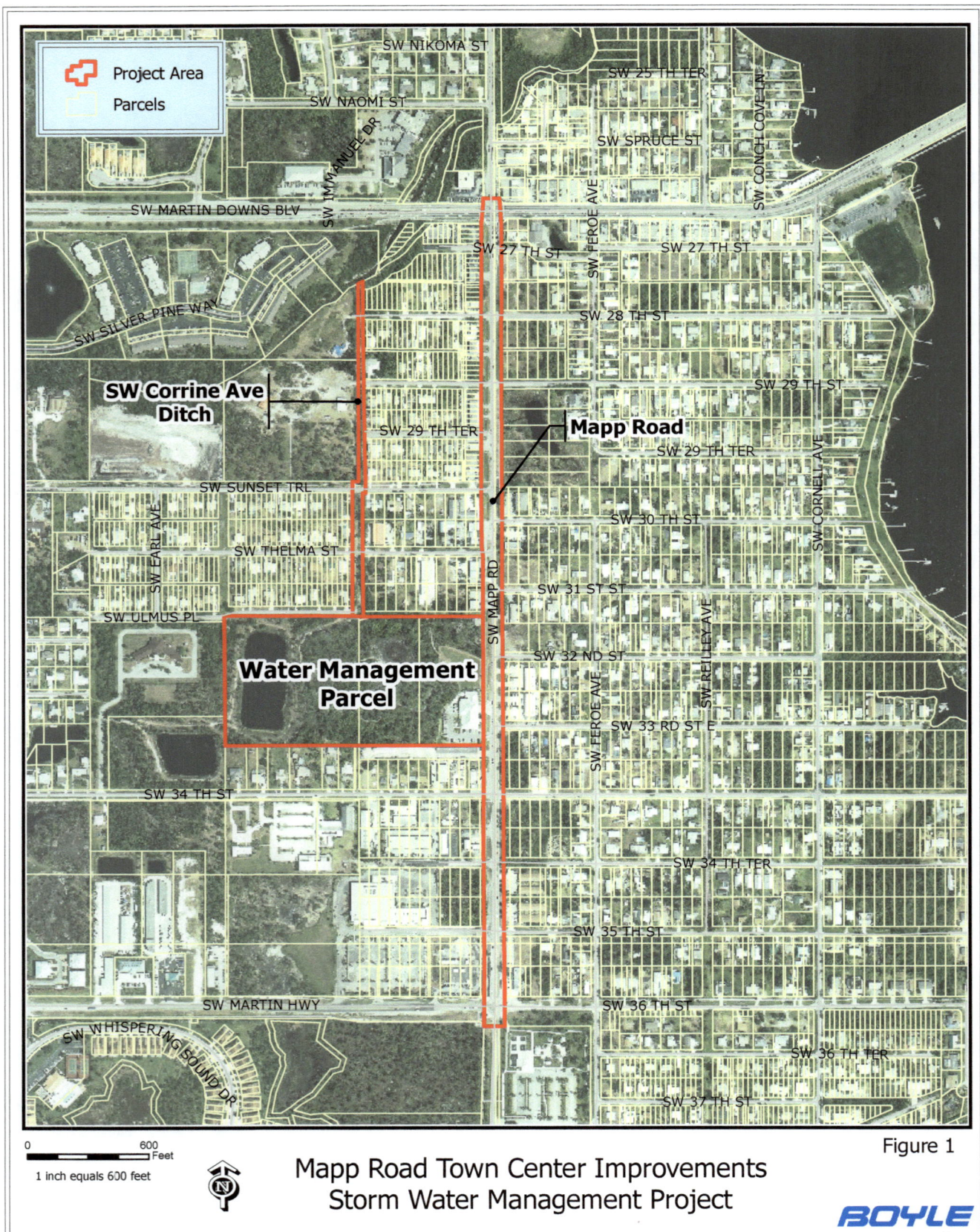

Mapp Road Town Center Improvements
Storm Water Management Project

Figure 1

1 inch equals 600 feet

0   600 Feet

13

Stormwater Permit

The master stormwater permit provided a solution for the stormwater issues for Mapp Road. The permit allowed for the construction of a combination of wet and dry stormwater management system. The permit required the restoration of historic wetlands, and connected to several existing systems. This marvel of engineering would create an almost 20 acre stormwater management parcel on Mapp Road within the Mixed-Use overlay.

The proposed system would collect all of the stormwater for Mapp Road from Martin Downs to Martin Highway, and pipe it to center of Mapp Road. The large amount of land was required for this system due to the outfall constraints of the Danforth Creek.

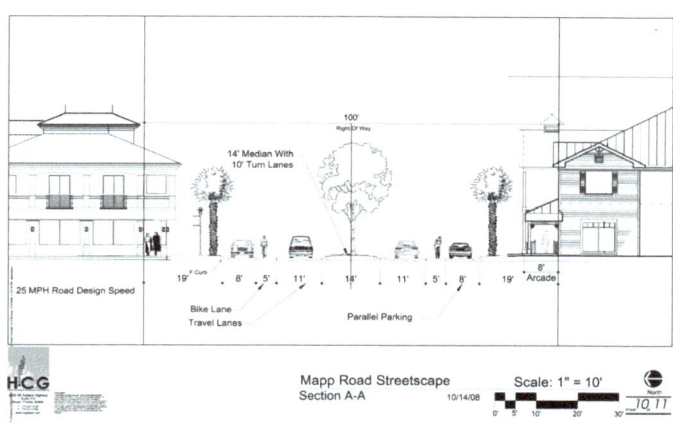

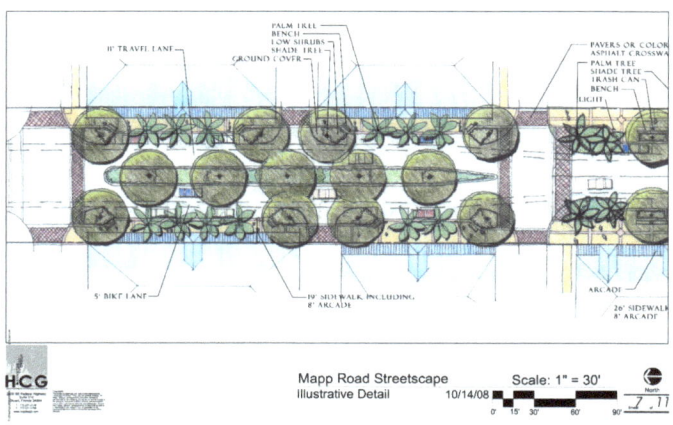

Above *These are the possible roadway sections for Mapp Road that were developed as a result of the Community redevelopment plan.*
Left Top *This illustration shows the composition and size of the proposed stormwater parcel. The large wet pond, shown in blue, is required to hold the stormwater from Mapp Road, until it could be slowly discharged into the Danforth Creek.*

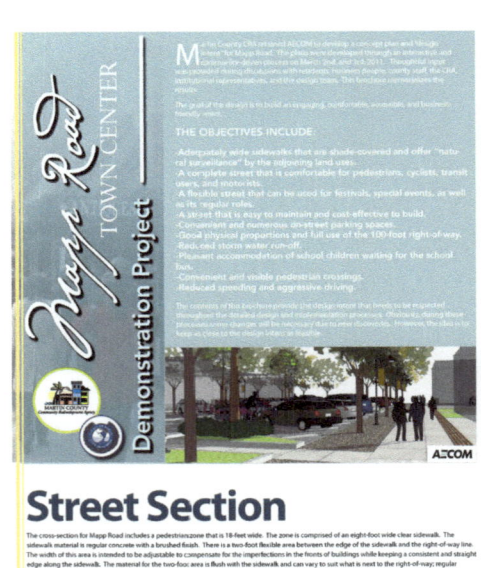

Street Section

Back-in Angled Parking

Curbless Street

Valley Gutter/Bike Lane

Water Strategies

Top: *All of the ideas from the community workshop were organized on a project board that was distributed throughout the community. This poster was also printed on a 4x8 billboard and posted on the corridor at the intersection of Sunset Trail.*

Above and Left: *Mapp Road property owners opened a shop front for the use of a community studio where residents could participate in the engineering for Mapp Road. Engineers met with residents, business owners, and County Staff over several days.*

Design

With the stormwater permits in hand, and the community support from the NOW Visioning, the CRA authorized a contract with AECom to develop a demonstration design for Mapp Road in March 2011. This design work was assigned to the Martin County Engineering Department to manage, and included the cost to build the stormwater treatment parcel and a portion of the Mapp Road from SW Ulmas St to SW 29th Terrace (1,100 linear feet) (Contract for $310,000)

This planning included a community workshop held in a shop front on Mapp Road. Residents, property owners, county staff, and the franchise utility providers, participated in the workshop. Through this process, consensus was formed for the proposed roadway section which minimized the disruption to local businesses. The design also included several cost construction savings recommendations such as utilizing the existing pavement of Mapp Road.

As the design progressed in November 2011, the cost estimate exceeded the budget and available Tax Increment Funding (TIF). This required some value engineering such as eliminating undergrounding utilities portion of the project. The estimated cost for this first phase of the project was $2,043,585 for small roadway section and stormwater treatment area.

In February 2012, the 100% design completed for the demonstration project. At this same time, the Community Development Department hired a project engineer familiar with roadway retrofits. Community Development Staff began analyzing the design in search of additional cost savings. Staff found that existing stormwater treatment areas and existing pipes currently accommodates existing stormwater on Mapp Road. Staff also explored strategies and materials in the stormwater toolkit to find innovative treatment strategies to reduce overall costs to allow more of the roadway to be improved. These new findings began to eliminate the high costs and need for the stormwater treatment parcel.

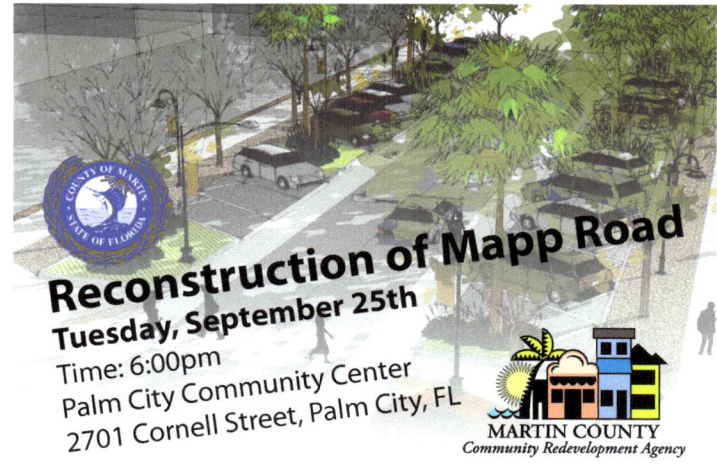

The Community Redevelopment Agency began seeking additional funding sources through grants in August 2012. These grants would provide the funding to construct the entire stormwater treatment area. Half of the stormwater treatment area is outside of CRA boundary, so funding would have to be a source other than TIF.

By September 2012, the CRA was notified that the various grants were not awarded. Community Development Staff continued to research seeking the best way to maximize TIF funds, and implement the Mapp Road Project. This required staff to explore ideas outside the box.

Maximizing the Benefit

Nov 2012 – Staff reviewed current budget and what amenities could be built for the entire stretch of Mapp Road. The majority of the project cost was dedicated to stormwater management, and this work would be underground or on parcels away from Mapp Road.

This challenged staff to explore innovate engineering solutions that focused the project back onto Mapp Road. Staff organized the community into several categories, and assigned projected project cost to each improvement.

Staff invited the community to a workshop where staff shared this information and explained every possible improvement that could be included on Mapp Road. Residents were asked to prioritize the top improvements for Mapp Road.

This input was critical in the process, because the community overwhelming demanded that the project needed to impact the entire corridor.

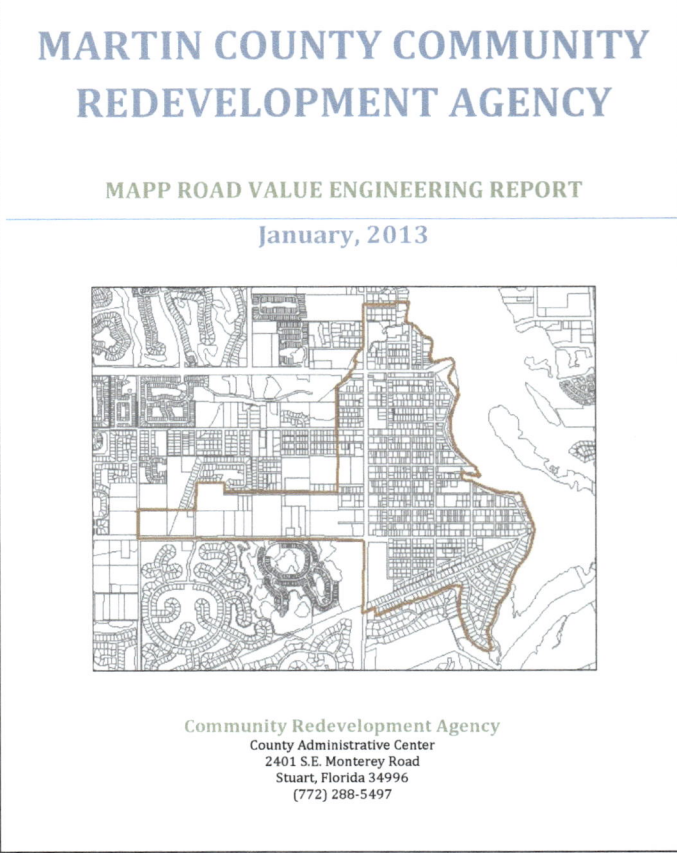

MARTIN COUNTY COMMUNITY REDEVELOPMENT AGENCY

MAPP ROAD VALUE ENGINEERING REPORT

January, 2013

Community Redevelopment Agency
County Administrative Center
2401 S.E. Monterey Road
Stuart, Florida 34996
(772) 288-5497

Above: *Staff prepared a report to value engineer the project so that the project could be constructed within available Tax Increment Financing.*

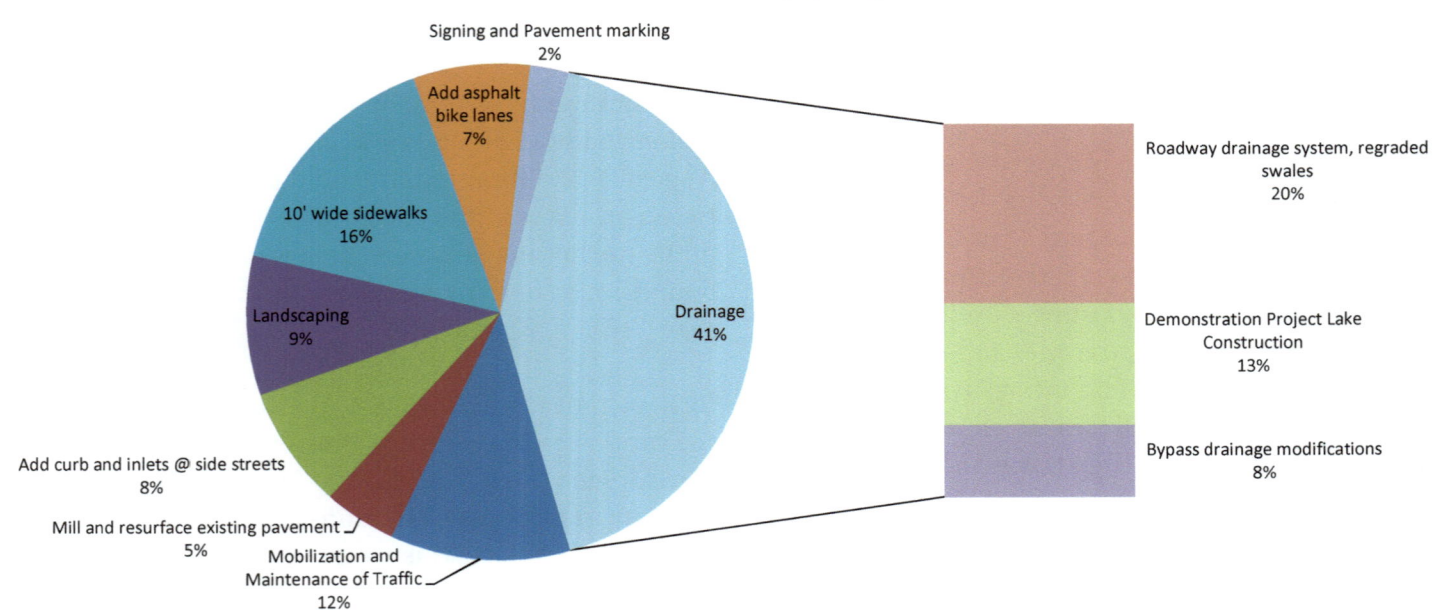

**Mapp Road Town Center Value Engineering Proposal
Total Construction cost $1,261,000**

- Signing and Pavement marking 2%
- Add asphalt bike lanes 7%
- 10' wide sidewalks 16%
- Landscaping 9%
- Add curb and inlets @ side streets 8%
- Mill and resurface existing pavement 5%
- Mobilization and Maintenance of Traffic 12%
- Drainage 41%
  - Roadway drainage system, regraded swales 20%
  - Demonstration Project Lake Construction 13%
  - Bypass drainage modifications 8%

WANTED
MAPP ROAD
REWARD
YOUR INPUT

Public Meeting 6pm 11/19
PALM CITY
COMMUNITY CENTER

Top: *Flyers were distributed throughout the community.*
Right: *Residents were presented with every element that could be included on Mapp Road and prioritized the most important elements.*

Colored Bike Lanes

Furniture/bike racks

Landscape/trees

Mid Block Crossing

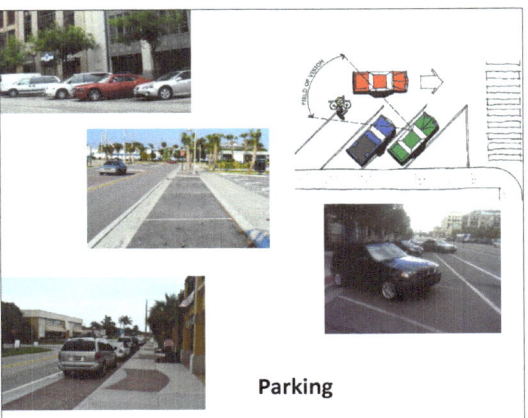

Parking

Rain Gardens/Bio Swales

Roundabouts

Textured Crosswalks

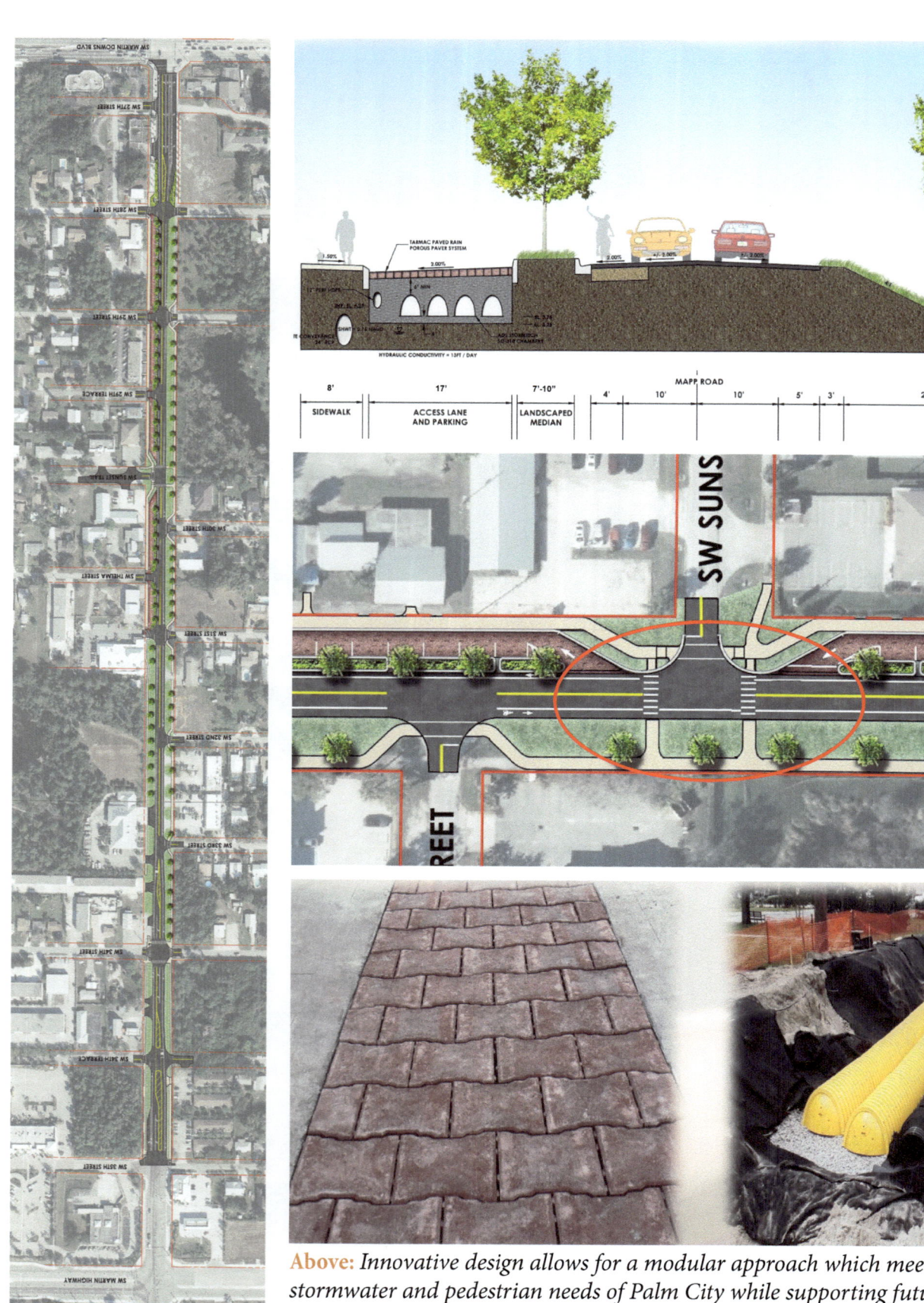

Above: *Innovative design allows for a modular approach which meet the immediate stormwater and pedestrian needs of Palm City while supporting future private redevelopment investment on Mapp Road.*

Modular Design and Implementation

December 2013 – Agreement with Kimley Horn to prepare Concept Plan for Mapp Road (Contract for $23,700)

- 2013 TAP Grant for FY 16-17 projects - Applied for grant - Received $234,400 for bike lanes

February 2014 – Concept design approved by the NAC

- Proposed a modular approach with components being built as funding allows. The primary aim of the design will be to eliminate the costs that would be incurred with the construction of the traditional stormwater piping and detention/retention areas
- Proposed improvements from SW 35th Street to Martin Downs Blvd (exisitng and proposed ROW = 100 feet; 3,600 linear feet; 35 properties)
- Project objectives: multi-modal facilities; improved parking accomodations; landscape improvements; innovative stormwater solutions; visible improvemetns for entire corridor; modular design flexibility
- Existing swale storage volume = .25 acre/feet @ Elevation 6.0 NAVD
- Proposed porous paver storage volume = .50 acre/feet @ Elevation 6.0 NAVD

April 2014 – Agreement with Kimley Horn to prepare full design plans (Contract for $174,020)

August 2014 – 50% construction plans

- Property owner coordination meetings

November 2014 – NAC approved the project design and five modular design elements

January 2015 – 90% construction plans
February 2015 – Did not receive FDEP grant

(requested $600,000) for storm water improvements (pollutant load reduction)

- With limited budget, phasing of the project is required.
- NAC approved the project as proposed in two phases: Phase I will consists of realignment of Mapp Road, resurfacing, bike lanes, swales reconfiguration, pipe connection, crosswalks, landscaping, and sidewalk connection. Phase II will consist of modular pieces and will be constructed as additional funding become available.

Implementation

Incremental Implementation

The Community Redevelopment Plan establishes a long term community vision for the future of the redevelopment area. The Community Development Department seeks opportunities to advance this vision with each capital investment through adaptive innovation. This lean approach to infrastructure supports the implementation of the community vision incrementally over time.

Mapp Road Sidewalk

In 2010, the Community Development Department collaborated with the Engineering Department, leveraging TIF dollars to enhance a standard traffic management project with the installation of wider sidewalks and substantial streetscape at Mapp Road and Martin Downs Boulevard. These improvements were the first section constructed for the ultimate vision for Mapp Road, and created a signature entry feature to Mapp Road.

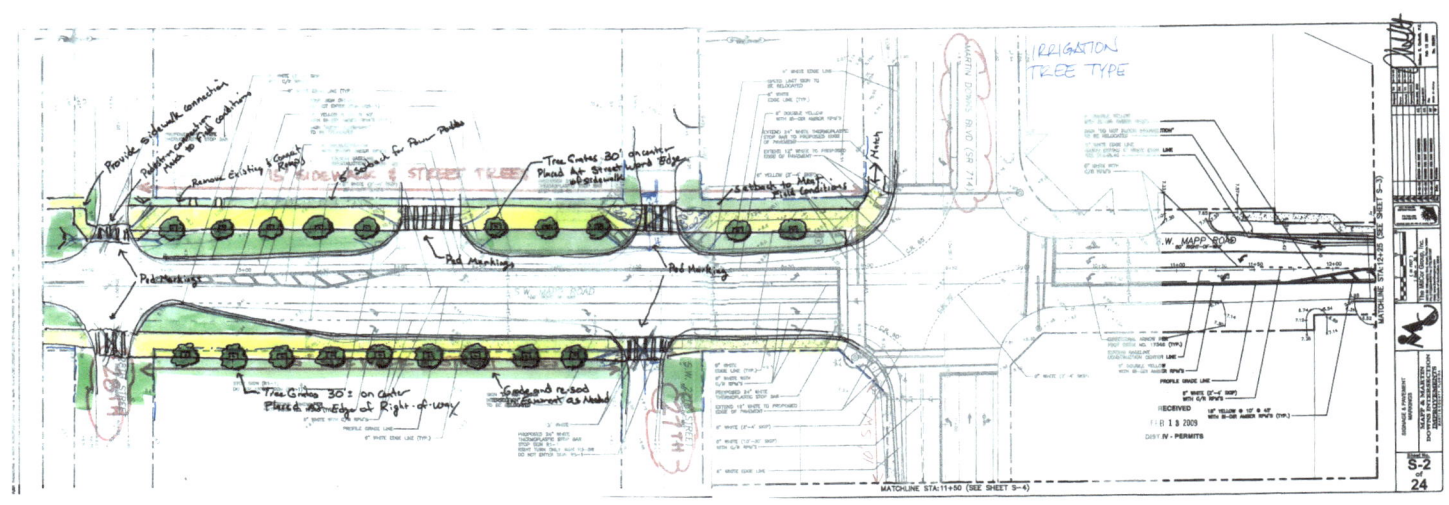

PARKING AND
TRANSPORTATION
IN COMMUNITY
REDEVELOPMENT
AREAS

A case study of the Hobe Sound
and Old Palm City CRAs

September, 2006

Parking Study

In 2006, Community Development Department Staff evaluated the parking needs for the redevlopment areas following the principles promoted by famed University of California Professor, Donald Shoup. Shoup's work book "The High Cost of Free Parking," had recently been published which explains how better parking policies can improve cities, the economy, and the environment.

This report outlined a series of key elements needed to implement transportation improvements that are part of the Palm City and Hobe Sound Redevelopment Plans. Such improvements include:

- Generous sidewalks
- Shade trees, benches, and awnings to make the sidewalk more inviting
- Less on-site parking and less of it visible from the main street
- More on-street parking, shared parking among several businesses, parking lots and parking garages
- Encourage more people to walk or bicycle to the downtown area
- Encourage people to park once and walk to multiple stores or offices
- Encourage more compact development and discourage the unnecessary use of increasingly valuable land for surface parking.

The parking study also highlighted the need to create a unified parking code with shared and reduced parking rates for redevelopment, the establishment of a parking trust fund, and utilizing public rights of way for on-street parking to meet redevelopment parking requirements.

This report was shared with the Neighborhood Advisory Committees, local businesses, and local chamber of commerce. These ideas were also implemented into the Martin County Land Code, and utilized in the redevelopment of parcels in the Community Redevelopment Areas.

Existing parking	
Bridge Road	278
Dixie frontage road	135
Dixie Highway	55
FEC ROW	30
Neighborhood streets	18
Total	516

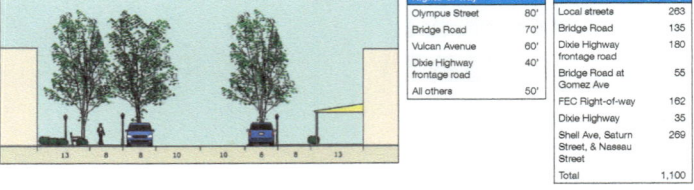

Rights-of-way	
Olympus Street	80'
Bridge Road	70'
Vulcan Avenue	60'
Dixie Highway frontage road	40'
All others	50'

Potential on-street parking	
Local streets	263
Bridge Road	135
Dixie Highway frontage road	180
Bridge Road at Gomez Ave	55
FEC Right-of-way	162
Dixie Highway	35
Shell Ave, Saturn Street, & Nassau Street	269
Total	1,100

Above *Exerts from the parking study specific to the Community Redevelopment Overlays for Hobe Sound, including the inventory of existing parking and possible parking configurations.*

Demonstration Rain Garden

As part of the Mapp Road Improvements project, a small demonstration rain garden was designed and installed on the east side of Mapp Road just north of SW 28th Street to receive runoff from hard surfaces such as sidewalk and roadway. This attractive, environmentally-friendly project allows water to infiltrate into the soil rather than becoming runoff. This helps to protect the quality of water downstream by preventing runoff from entering storm drains and helps reduce the chances for local flooding.

Rain gardens give stormwater a chance to slowly seep into the groundwater instead of rushing into storm drains all at once. In addition, rain gardens help to reduce the amount of sediment and other pollutants that runoff typically carries into drainage systems.

The rain garden was installed by Valley Crest Landscaping and was funded through Tax Increment Financing (TIF) funds.

Project Type:
- Innovative Stormwater Management

Funding Source:
- Staff Time
- Tax Increment Financing (TIF) $8,250

Status:
- Completed

Project Manager: Pinal Gandhi-Savdas

Private Sector Investment

PALM CITY ANIMAL MEDICAL CENTER

Development for 13,728 square foot, one-story, animal clinic, including grooming and boarding facilities and accommodations, on a 0.859 acre parcel located at the northeast corner of the intersection of Mapp Rd. and Ulmus Place in Palm City.

This Development Order Signed June 2009, and the doors opened in December 2010. This was the first new commercial development constructed under the Zoning Overlay which requires building built to the street, with the parking on the side and rear. This development was designed for the ultimate roadway section, and contributed funds to the CRA for improvements on Mapp Road.

MAPP ROAD SUNOCO

This gas station replaced a station destroyed during the 2004 hurricanes, and the redevelopment was required to meet the requirements of the zoning overlay. The retail portion of the operation is built to the street with a front porch and entry off Mapp Road. This Sunoco was the second new development approved on Mapp Road, and the front porch has become the official morning coffee shop in the community.

This site was developed in coordination with the Martin County Engineering Department for proper alignment with the sidewalk. This construction occurred in advance of the roadway work. This development paid the County for the required right of way landscaping which the county will install with the implementation of Mapp Road.

PALM CITY SHOPPES

This development application for 17,900 square foot retail, restaurant and bank development on a 1.51 acre parcel located on Mapp Road, and has been designed for the future section of Mapp Road. The Development Order signed June 2011, and construction has not started. this development Contributed $5,000 towards future landscaping on Mapp Road.

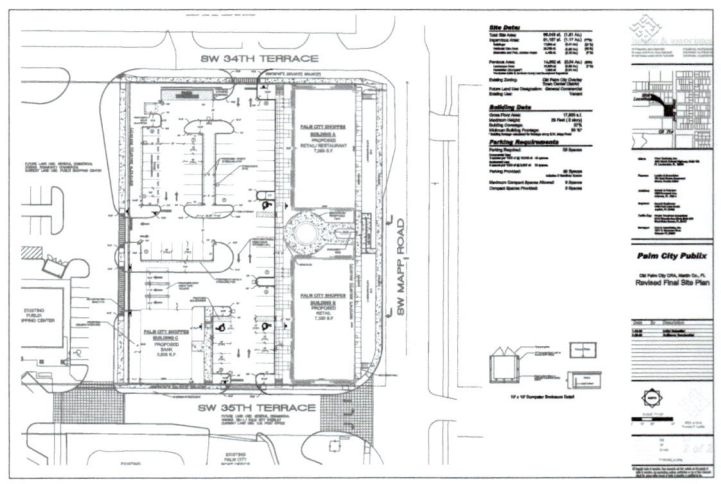

Property Appraisal Evaluation

The Community Redevelopment Agency annually maps the appraised and taxable property values as assigned by the Martin County Property Appraiser in each of the redevelopment areas. These maps illustrate the wealth and productivity found in the community redevelopment areas. Staff is also able to evaluate the property tax implications of different development types and the return on investment for capital projects.

According to the Property Appraiser, the seven Martin County Community Redevelopment Areas have a combined appraised value of $1.1 billion, of which $736 million is taxable. The CRA encompasses 8,500 acres of land mass or about 3% of the County. The value of taxable of the land within the CRA is some of the most productive land representing over 5% of the total taxable value for Martin County.

The analysis for Old Palm City illustrate the potential for the increase of the values along Mapp Road in conjunction with public investment. The majority of properties on Mapp Road today are vacant. Recent redevelopments such as the Palm City Animal Medical Center, have had exponential increases the value per acre.

This redevelopment included the demolition of an existing structure, was built to the current redevelopment standards, and approved in conjunction with the proposed design of Mapp Road. In addition to the increase value of this property, the adjacent existing development also increased in value. The value per acre as reported by the Martin County Property Appraiser exceeds the valuation of all other parcels in Palm City, including other commercial properties on the water.

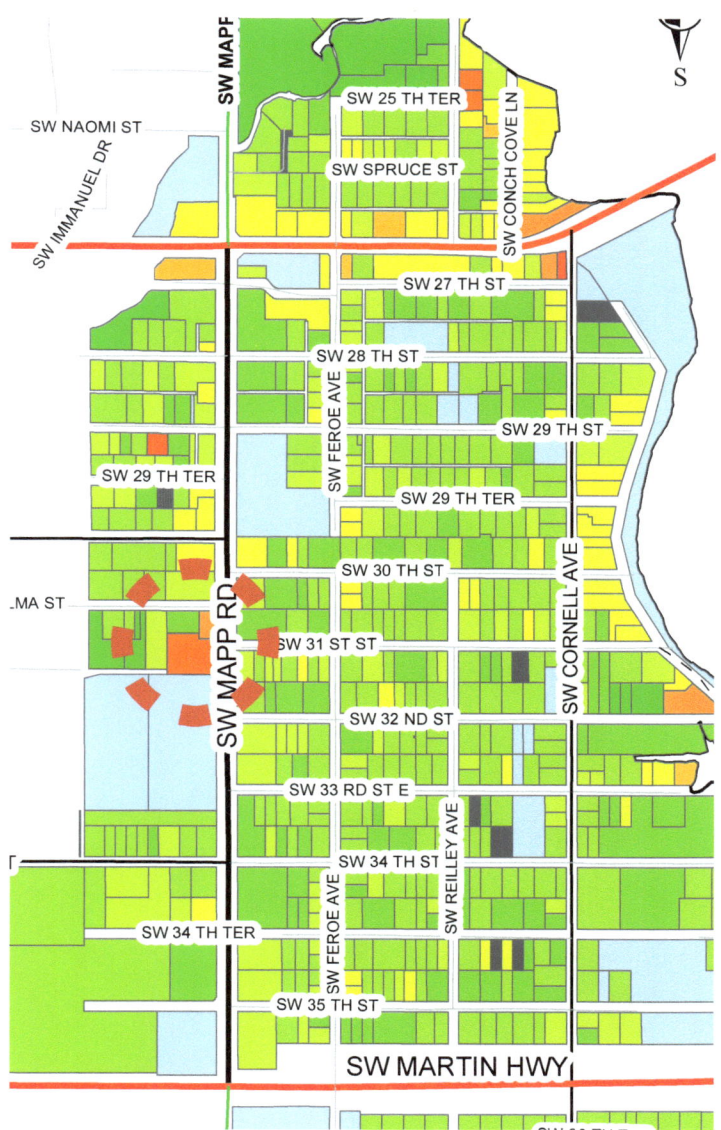

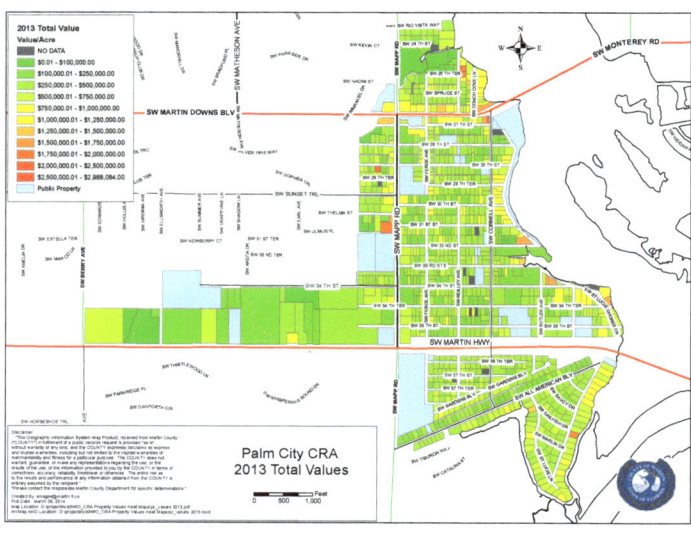

Palm City CRA
2013 Total Values